Images of
SOUTHAMPTON

Images of
SOUTHAMPTON

Alastair Arnott
and Rachel Wragg

First published in Great Britain by The Breedon Books Publishing Company Limited
44 Friar Gate, Derby, DE1 1DA. 1994. Softback edition 2006.

This paperback edition published in Great Britain in 2013 by DB Publishing,
an imprint of JMD Media Ltd

© Southampton City Council

ISBN 978-1-78091-318-6

Printed and bound in the UK by Copytech (UK) Ltd Peterborough

Contents

Introduction

THE illustrations used in compiling *Images of Southampton*, come almost exclusively from the collections of Southampton City Heritage Services; credit is given below for those that are from other sources. In bringing them together, we have tried to present as balanced a view of the development of Southampton as possible, while showing some of the range and variety of illustrative material which is available from the City's own resources. This book therefore forms something of a 'shop window' on our wares.

What has been available for selection has inevitably depended on what has survived, and of this, what the public has entrusted to our care. We hope that individuals will continue to furnish us with historically significant material, so that it can be preserved for future generations.

It is widely known that Southampton City Heritage holds the extensive Associated British Ports Photographic Collection, so it may surprise some readers that this has not been more extensively used. Much of it, however, was felt to be too specialised for inclusion; working on this same principle we have tried to moderate the effect which our own interests and enthusiasms could have on a book like this.

Pictures don't tell the whole story. The Roman settlement of Clausentum is reputed to have been in the area of Bitterne. Later, separate habitations were established by the Saxons at Hamwic, and in Medieval times, within the precincts of the surviving walls. Thus a recurring phenomenon was established, of phases of considerable importance in the economy of the nation, alternating with periods of relative obscurity. Two of these cycles, the Spa period and the period of the Ocean Liner, are probably most evident from the illustrations chosen.

During the Spa period, Southampton was popularised by Prince Frederick of Wales, the eldest son of George II, and his three sons. Not only were many elegant buildings erected and country houses built, but the town itself was transformed. There was considerable building outside the walls, gas street lighting was introduced, and the railway arrived, linking Southampton with London.

Later on it was the railway which gave the impetus for the founding of the docks, although the two developments were originally seen as separate projects. Thus, as the prosperity of the spa town faded, Southampton began to blossom as a port for the recently-perfected steam ship. The day of the ocean liner had dawned. Communications rapidly developed to all parts of the Empire and beyond, causing Southampton to be known by the slogan on a Southern Railway poster, as the 'Gateway to the World'.

After World War Two, the coming of fast and efficient aircraft put paid to the reign of the great liners, still fondly remembered by many. The bustle and glamour may have gone, but ferries and cruise ships use the port in growing numbers, and a greater volume of cargo is handled than ever before. There is a considerable industrial base, and several new commercial developments are rejuvenating the city centre, which had suffered some rather drab post-war rebuilding. Our ancient monuments are cherished and preserved; our glorious parks and open spaces, nurtured over the years, continue to give pleasure to all. There will be much for future picture researchers to present.

This work could not have been completed without assistance. We would therefore like to record our thanks to:- John Lawrence, for his photographic work; volunteers Dora Caton and Margaret Ball, for their valuable knowledge and assistance; and our hard-pressed colleagues June McGee and Jill Neale, for interpreting the text. The assistance of the following in respect of certain of the photographs should also be acknowledged: Southern Newspapers; the Royal Engineers' Museum; Pirelli General; and Donald S. Herbert. The authors would also like to take this opportunity to apologise to anyone whose name has inadvertently been left out; we are profoundly grateful to you all.

ALASTAIR ARNOTT
RACHEL WRAGG
Southampton
September 1994

Introduction to the Second Edition

I AM grateful to all those local historians and Southampton enthusiasts for the helpful and constructive comments that were received when this book was first published. Virtually all their suggestions have been incorporated here.

It would be invidious to single out any individual for his assistance, but I am particularly grateful to Alan Morton for his painstaking and meticulous compilation of the Topographical Index. This should be of benefit to all those who need a particular image.

Time of course does not stand still and further revision of the text has been necessary because of changes that have taken place within the City. Arundel Towers are no more and their site has been incorporated into the vast West Quay shopping complex. The Gas Column continues its peripatetic journey round Southampton.

The Museum collections on which the book is based, have not yet caught up with these changes, but that does not detract from the use of historical material and I hope that more people will now be able to enjoy these glimpses of a bygone age.

Alastair Arnott,
July, 2006.

Foreword

THIS book is a tribute to the courage and resilience of the Southampton people and an attempt to capture the way in which they have worked together, with fortitude and dignity, through turbulent times to create the modern, bustling and vibrant European city of which we can all be proud.

The ancient walls of the medieval town are strongly in evidence. Thanks to restoration work undertaken by the City Council, in consultation with English Heritage, they will remain a distinguishing feature of Southampton into the twenty-first century and beyond. A novel interpretative scheme known as "Walk the Walls", has been put in place to make them accessible to all. Without such a scheme, the walls would have remained a closed book to many.

Similar projects in the former docks areas, which are themselves being redeveloped for leisure and commercial purposes, will extend this facility and allow everyone to learn about and to enjoy their past.

All of our local authority museums; Tudor House, Woolhouse and God's House Tower, feature in this book because their structures are also ancient monuments. Again we are proud to play a leading role in preserving the character of the city, and making the buildings and their collections serve the needs of local inhabitants. Surveys have shown an increasing awareness of, and appetite for, heritage related subjects within broad sections of the community.

Many of the illustrations in this book have been donated to City Heritage Services by local people, and show parts of the city which the donors knew and for which they clearly felt considerable affection. We hope that in making this selection we can share with others the treasures which we hold in trust for the future, and open more of our heritage for study and enjoyment.

Councillor John Truscott

Within And Around The Walls

THIS section looks at the area of the town from the Bargate to Town Quay, and the area just outside the walls linking the original medieval town to its Regency and Victorian neighbours.

The medieval town was surrounded by impressive defensive walls, about a mile and a quarter in circumference, with gates and posterns at several points. The historian Englefield in his *Walk through Southampton,* published in 1801, traced their foundation to the time of Edward II, although parts of the wall are undoubtedly older than this. The Bargate provided a grand entrance to the town, leading into the main street, or English Street, as it was known throughout the Middle Ages. French Street, running parallel to the west, was the quarter of the town occupied by French settlers. Other gates providing access to the town included the Water Gate, which stood at the bottom of the High Street and was demolished in 1804, the East Gate, pulled down in 1776, and the West Gate and God's House Gate, both of which still exist.

The lack of a complete defensive wall made possible the attack by combined French and Genoese forces in 1338, which resulted in an orgy of pillage and slaughter, together with considerable damage by fire. The King, Edward III, lost a substantial quantity of wine and wool from the royal vaults of the castle during the assault. Following the subsequent inquiry the town was instructed to complete its defences in order to prevent further attacks from the seaward side.

Even allowing for the scourge of the Black Death which struck the town in 1348, progress in completing the wall was slow, as many merchants had properties facing the western shore and were reluctant to see them demolished. The eventual result was the construction of a unique arcaded wall in front of the houses, the dwellings simply being incorporated into the new stonework. By 1385 the main circuit of the town's defences was virtually complete, with the names of the two leading protagonists, Sir John Arundel and John Polymond, being commemorated in the names of the north-west and north-east towers respectively.

Sir John Arundel was commander of Southampton Castle, a royal castle of some importance and a dominant feature of this part of the town. Norman in origin, it too underwent alterations following the French raid, but later fell into disrepair, and by the late sixteenth century cattle were reported to be grazing in its precincts. In 1605 King James I sold it. The Marquis of Lansdowne purchased the site in 1805, and built a spectacular mock castle, known as 'Lansdowne's Folly' which was demolished *c.*1820. Today only fragments of the original buildings survive, while a block of flats has been erected on the site of the Norman bailey.

Throughout the centuries the character of this, the oldest part of the town, changed radically. The water reached right up Western Shore until the land was reclaimed in 1910, although the focus of maritime activity had already moved with the opening of modern deep-water docks in 1838. The merchants houses fell out of use, and a myriad of small dwellings, pubs and lodging houses developed, often clustered around little courts, with no proper drainage or sewerage. The threat of a cholera epidemic was constant in these overcrowded wards, where the population was 441.4 per acre in 1890, compared to Portswood, where the figure was only 14.5. A report by the Borough Medical Officer of Health, published in 1894, persuaded the Corporation to adopt a redevelopment scheme for the worst slum areas between Blue Anchor Lane, Simnel Street and Castle Lane. This scheme, which included dwellings for artisans and a model lodging house in St Michael's Square, was completed in 1903.

Dissecting the old town, the High Street begins at the Bargate and runs right down to Town Quay. John Leland, visiting the town in the 1540s, described it as 'one of the fairest streets that is in any town in England'. As the main street of the town, this was where the majority of the wealthy merchants houses were situated during the medieval period. The narrow fronted, timber-framed houses usually consisted of three chambers: a central hall, with a separate room at either end. These were normally constructed over a stone-built vault or semi-basement, used for warehousing and storage. The best surviving example of this type of construction is the 'medieval Merchants House' at 58 French Street, although German bombing raids during World War Two brought to light many more examples of the stone-vaulted basements which have been preserved in the lower portion of the High Street.

The Bargate marked the entrance into the medieval walled town from the north. Probably beginning as a wooden structure shortly after the Norman Conquest, it was increasingly well fortified throughout the Middle Ages. By the twelfth century a triple stone arch had been erected, and a century or so later drum towers were added on either side. In the fifteenth century it became the seat of local government when the Guildhall was established in one of the central towers, and it continued in use as a law court until the Civic Centre law courts were opened in 1933.

A pair of lions, originally with lamps in their mouths, stood either side of the gate to guide visitors towards it. The first set were old in 1619 when the Corporation paid to have them varnished, while the present lions were presented by William Lee when he was made a Burgess of the town in 1774. Until the nineteenth century the north front of Bargate also displayed the coats of arms of prominent local families, and two painted wooden panels depicting Sir Bevois, the legendary Southampton knight, and his adversary, the giant Ascupart. The south front still houses the statue of George III, dressed as the Roman Emperor Hadrian, which was placed there by the second Marquis of Lansdowne in 1809.

In 1771 the town pavement commissioners resolved to 'improve the beauty and convenience of the High Street', resulting in the gradual disappearance of the narrow medieval timber frontages. The Audit House, which had stood in the centre of the road opposite Holyrood Church, was demolished and rebuilt on the opposite side of the street, providing the town with a magnificent new town hall, but burdening the Corporation with a debt of some £4,000. Many medieval buildings were either demolished or substantially rebuilt in line with the vogue for classical architecture. Brick or stone front elevations with large windows, often bowed like those of the Dolphin Hotel, became the norm. All Saints Church, on the corner of the High Street and East Street, was rebuilt in 1795 and was dominated by a classical Ionic colonnade on its street frontage. Both paved and illuminated by 1782, the character of the High Street was becoming recognisably modern.

Below Bar was still the commercial heart of the town, and businesses and shops thrived. The rather dull Georgian shop windows, in which nothing but boxes were displayed and the customer had to request sight of the goods, were gradually replaced by their Victorian equivalents, displaying a huge amount and variety of stock, often hung outside the door and on street awnings when space became too restricted inside. Although customer accounts were still common enough, the age of 'cash' shopping was beginning to arrive. Several banks had premises on the High Street, including a branch of the Bank of England, although the National and Provincial (now the National Westminster) at No.129 was probably the oldest.

It was reputed to have the longest banking counter in the country in the 1860s, and must have been a sign of the prosperity of the town. Further down, the Hartley Institution with its spectacular Portland stone facade provided a cultural centre and seat of learning for the town, which was to become a University College in 1902.

Although an 1896 guide book to Southampton still described the High Street as retaining a great 'many quaint erections', it was a modern, bustling thoroughfare terminating at Town Quay, where large numbers of vessels loaded and discharged a huge variety of cargo, all of which stimulated and enriched the local economy.

A mid-nineteenth-century trade plate by Philip Brannon advertising the services of Alfred Pegler. In addition to producing jewellery and this ornamental table piece, which was presented to the mayor George Lashley, Peglers were also a manufacturing gunsmith. *LSH 781*

The home of Henry Robinson Hartley who founded the Hartley Institute by bequest in 1850. This was "established to promote the study and advancement of the Sciences of Natural History, Astronomy, Antiquities, and Classical and Oriental Literature in the town of Southampton." The original Hartley Institute building was opened on this site in the High Street, by Lord Palmerston, in 1862.

An exhibition of material collected from throughout the British Empire, held at the Hartley Institute in July 1866. Exhibitions of this nature were regularly held during the summer and the institute had a large collection of its own artefacts, which eventually formed the basis of the collection given to display at Southampton's first museum in 1912.

High Street, Below Bar c. 1900. On the right is the Hartley Institute identifiable by the four figures surrounding the doorway. The Hartley Institute became a University College in 1902 and after World War I, moved to a much larger site in Highfield.

A busy scene just Below Bar in the 1890s with a horse tram passing under Bargate. All the buildings on both sides of the road, including the reconstructed and enlarged church of All Saints, were lost during the Blitz of 1940. *54/1254*

The High Street *c.*1905, still clearly the centre of commercial activity with the Bargate in the distance. The Corporation took over the tramway system in 1898 and immediately set about modernising it; the High Street route was the first to be electrified in January 1900. *54/64*

This shows the Southampton Times Building on the corner of Pound Tree Road, with the Royal Hotel next door. Opposite, and nearest the camera in the bottom right, is the roof of the Church of Christ (Above Bar Church) with the Philharmonic Hall adjacent to it.

The port of Southampton has been of major military importance since at least the fourteenth century. During World War One a total of seven million officers and men passed through the town.

Edwin Jones came to Southampton from Romsey in the 1830s and began a small drapery business in East Street. He was later able to open one of the first true 'department' stores at 1-9 Queens Buildings, pictured below, which was described in a 1892 directory as 'wholesale warehousemen, silk mercers, drapers and provision merchants.' *M5811*

High Street in the early 1930s. The Westminster Bank, now the National Westminster Bank, still occupies the same site at no. 12. although the original building was lost during World War II. The Gaiety Cinema on the other side of the road was the last cinema to be opened in Southampton before the commencement of World War I, and the first to show "talkies". It remained in independent ownership until closure in April, 1956.

Southampton suffered its worst bombing raids of World War II, in November and December 1940. This burned out tram in Bernard Street illustrates the devastation caused by the bombing in what became known as the Southampton "blitz".

This is the aftermath, although the rubble has been removed and fencing erected to prevent accidents.

High Street, Below Bar looking towards Town Quay at the crossroads of High Street, St Michaels Street and Bridge Street (now Bernard Street). This picture, taken in the 1890s, shows that the commercial focus of the town was still situated well Below Bar with businesses ranging from Cranbrook's Jewellers at No.126 and Cooksey's Export Provision Merchants at 125 to the Nags Head and General Post Office on the opposite side of the street.

Medieval chimney at the back of a warehouse on Lower High Street. It was the only part of the building to remain standing after the Blitz and was removed and re-erected in Tudor House Museum Garden where it still stands. *M6304*

The magnificent blue and white tiled building of Oakley and Watling, Seedsmen, Fruiterers and Florists at 118 High Street remains one of the finest examples of Victorian architecture in the town. Next door is the Red Lion public house which began life as a medieval merchants house and still retains the fourteenth-century vaults. The courtroom is associated with the conspiracy against Henry V in 1415 and it is reputed that the trial of the conspirators took place here. *M6326*

Rebuilding the High Street after the German bombing raids of World War II. The Dolphin Hotel was damaged but survived, however Holy Rood church on the right of the photograph took a direct hit on 2 December, 1940 and was reduced to a shell. It is now a memorial to the City's merchant seamen.

Holy Rood Chambers at 125 High Street was built in 1885 for use by members of the legal profession. It is one of the few buildings in the area to have survived the Blitz. *54/1337*

The 'provisions' business of Frederick Charles Yeoman in East Street, photographed *c.*1914. *M5193*

Canal Walk – also known as the "Ditches" – ran along the outside of the walls. It was reported that "anything" could be bought in this small street which was totally destroyed during the Blitz in 1940. *M2241*

The Bill for the construction of the Southampton and Salisbury Canal received the Royal assent in May 1795 and was intended to form part of a larger canal system linking Andover with Redbridge. It was opened to traffic in 1804, but was beset with financial difficulties and was filled in during 1846. Subsequent excavations such as those associated with the construction of the railway, revealed sections of the canal wall. This photograph shows workmen in the Strand in 1929 where the stonework of the canal can clearly be seen. *M4358*

The Bull's Head pub at 55 French Street, looking up Vyse Lane towards Wickham Court. This area was the subject of major slum clearance early in the 20th. Century, although the Bull's Head survived to be restored to its original medieval appearance by English Heritage.

Wickham Court, approached from French Street, was one of the many areas of poor housing and slum dwellings which were not included in the town's main water and sewerage systems. These insanitary conditions meant that the threat of a cholera epidemic was always present.

In 1674, Isaac Watts, preacher and composer of hymns, was born in this house in French Street. The building later became a post office, but has since been demolished following substantial bomb damage. Isaac Watts is commemorated by a memorial in Watts Park, and during the day, the Civic Centre clock chimes the first bars of one of one of his best-known hymns, *O God our Help in Ages Past*, every four hours.

French Street, around 1910, looking south towards Town Quay. The boys, all in school uniform, may have been attending St John's School.

Children playing in one of the alleys which ran between many of the houses and shops in the oldest parts of the town. Although the street is paved the drain can still be seen running down the centre. *M6449*

French Street is recognisable today by the presence of Eagle Warehouse, which once belonged to May and Wade the export grocers and still bears their name, and by the medieval Merchant's House seemingly under the spire of St Michael's Church. Between them is the Empire Palace Music Hall. The photographer took this shot from outside the fourteenth-century Weigh House which housed the weigh-beam used for weighing wool for export. *M5834*

Tudor Merchant Hall was Southampton's original market hall. Built in the early 1400s it used to stand in St Michael's Square, but was dismantled and re-erected on its present site next to the Westgate in 1634. The move was apparaently initiated following complaints from parishioners about the smell of fish which was sold there.

The roof and interior of Tudor Merchants Hall just prior to its renovation in the early 1970s. The beams were found to have been numbered at some time, presumably to make the roof easier to build. *M4157*

St Joseph's Roman Catholic Church in Bugle Street. The Georgian house on the left, which is the presbytery, was purchased in 1828 and the first St Joseph's constructed in the grounds in 1830. The present building, of cream brick and Caen stone, was consecrated in 1844 and was commenced to designs by A.W.N.Pugin, but only the chancel was completed to his plan. Much modified since, there is little of the Pugin element except for an altar. *M6391*

St Michael's Church *c.*1890 looking south along Castle Way. Of early Norman origin it is one of the finest surviving pre-reformation churches in the city. It's disproportionately high spire was constructed in 1745 as a navigation aid to shipping in Southampton water.

West Gate, approached from West Gate Street, controlled access to the town from the sea. The water came virtually to the gateway until the land on the other side of Western Esplanade was reclaimed. *M6462*

Tudor House, built around 1500 as a town house for Sir John Dawtrey, a merchant and Customs Controller of the town. This photograph, probably taken in 1900 prior to its purchase by Reginal Spranger, shows that it had become dilapidated and divided into several dwellings and businesses. Spranger restored it to its "Tudor" form and persuaded the Town Council to take over the building. It opened as Southampton's first Museum in 1912. *M6148*

A group of workmen on the roof of Tudor House Museum in the early 20th. Century After Reginald Spranger bought the house, he is reputed to have spent £800 on restoration.

Blue Anchor Lane about 1890, with the medieval half-timbered buildings still intact. It was originally known as Wytegods Lane, but was eventually renamed after the pub, the Blue Anchor, which stood at the bottom near the Quay. This view Is looking up the lane into St. Michael's Square.

Blue Anchor Lane, looking through the remains of the Postern Gate to West Quay. On the left is the medieval Merchants House known as King John's Palace. It dates from the twelfth century and confirms the substantial wealth of some of the town's tradesmen. The ground floor, with large openings directly on to West Quay, was for the storage of goods, while the upper floor contained the domestic chambers. The back wall of the house was incorporated into the town's defences during the fourteenth century. *M6142*

These defensive walls in West Quay were built following the French raid of 1338, the arcades being built over the front walls of the merchants' houses which originally lined the quay. The outlines of the doors and windows of some of these earlier buildings are still clearly visible behind the extra stonework of the arcades, the construction of which made the top of the wall wide enough for a walkway for sentries guarding the town.

The interior of the Long Rooms, just before demolition *c*.1898. They were built along the western shore, close to the baths, for the benefit of wealthy visitors; Jane Austen is reported to have danced here during her stay in the town between 1807 and 1809. Dancing was the most popular amusement of the Georgian gentry, so balls were held as often as three times a week throughout the summer season. The entertainment was a very formal affair, conducted by a Master of Ceremonies and rules were strictly enforced. Ladies were not permitted to dance in an apron, mittens or black gloves, while in 1774 gentlemen were refused admission for wearing boots or carrying a sword. *LSH 334*

Public Baths, Western Shore Road. During the eighteenth century Southampton became popular as a 'Spa' town, both due to the discovery of its mineral water spring at Blychenden, and the increased popularity of sea bathing. Frederick, Prince of Wales, declared the waters of Southampton to be "salubrious and invigorating" in 1750. These baths were established with the assistance of a grant of land from the town council in order to provide 'unrivalled facilities for summer and winter sea bathing for both ladies and gentleman'. The price of a cold bath was 6d but after 5pm the workmen of the town could bathe for the reduced price of 1d. *M6069*

The Chamber of Commerce and Corn Exchange building on Town Quay with the Castle Hotel, which incorporated part of the town walls, next door. The hotel closed in the late 1880s and later became offices. The structure did not survive the war. *M6270*

Gods House Tower and the Platform, part of the Town's medieval defences. In the eighteenth century the buildings were used as a gaol to house 'felons and debtors' and later, because of its proximity to Town Quay, for warehousing. In 1900 the area was still a popular waterside walk. The statue of Prince Albert can clearly be seen in the centre of the picture. It was removed during World War I.

Old Tower Inn at the junction of Bargate Street & Western Esplanade. When the inn was demolished it was discovered that it was propping up the Arundel Tower. Extensive repairs were needed. *M6466*

Winkle Street with a view through Gods House Gate to the platform beyond. On the left is St Julian's Church, founded in 1226 by Gervais le Riche, a merchant of the town, supposedly in atonement for his money laundering activities. The chapel was assigned to French Huguenot refugees in the sixteenth century and is now sometimes known as the French Church. *LSH 832*

The twelfth century Merchant's House, known as Canute's Palace, in Porter's Lane. Originally the ground floor provided storage space with accommodation combining a living and business room above, although this photograph was taken around 1900 when the building was occupied by a coal merchant. *M6266*

Alderman Dunsford (at the controls) with other councillors and their wives at the inauguration ceremony of Southampton's electric tram service in January 1900.

Bernard Street in the late nineteenth century, with Holy Rood Church on the right and St Michael's in the background. The bank in the centre of the photograph, then the National and Provincial, was one of the earliest to be established in the town; in the 1860s it was reputed to have had the longest banking counter in the country. *M6477*

Holy Rood Church at the junction of High Street, Bernard Street and St Michael's Street. There has been a church on this site since the twelfth century, although it was largely rebuilt in 1848-49 and is seen here at its Victorian best. After bombing during World War Two, only the shell and tower remained, which have now been preserved as a monument to the dead of the Merchant Navy. Behind the church stood the well-known firm of Lankester & Son, whose foundry produced many of the Southampton lampposts and drain covers. *M6504*

Oxford Street during the 1930s. On the right is the tailors, Miller Rainer Haysom, were most Merchant Navy officers in Southampton were fitted with their uniforms. The sailors' home can be seen in the background. *TH2.222*

The corner of Bridge Road looking down Orchard Lane before 1900. The tracks of the horse-drawn tram line running from Bernard Street on the left to Oxford Street, can be seen in the foreground. The entrance to Orchard Lane was moved in the late 1950s.

The Green Shield Stamp Shop, synonymous with 1970s shopping, on the corner of East Street and Orchard Lane. The parking meters are also becoming items of historic interest as the city is gradually phasing them out in favour of 'pay and display' parking. *54/746*

Houndwell Gardens was a Victorian terrace running from East Street to Hanover Buildings, near to Houndwell Park. It was gradually demolished to make way for commercial expansion in the centre of the town. *M6327*

Hendy's have been associated with cycles and early motor vehicles in Southampton since the 1890s. This early twentieth-century advertisement shows that in addition to manufacturing their own vehicles they could also supply 'complete outfits'. A heavy motoring coat often proved a necessity for the early open horseless carriages.

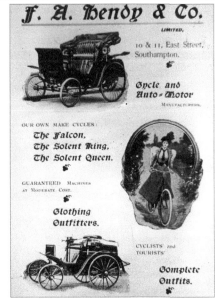

East Street *c.*1910 was the main shopping thoroughfare linking the St Mary's area of the town to the High Street. This busy scene shows many businesses, both large and small, which thrived here.

The roof of the South Western Hotel proved a great vantage point for photographers. Here the lines of the horse tramway can be seen turning from Oxford Street, by the Telegraph Office, into Terminus Terrace, and passing in front of Radley's Hotel. The houses of Queen's Terrace can also be seen on the left, over the roof of the South Western Hotel. *54/41*

A Hotchkiss machine gun for anti-aircraft defence was first mounted on Catchcold Tower overlooking the Pirelli Factory on Western Esplanade in 1940. This picture was taken in 1945 when American Service personnel and their vehicles were still much in evidence in the city. *LSH 471*

The Southampton works of Pirelli General in 1965. The 1913 factory can be seen fronting Western Esplanade. The Masonic Temple in Albion Place is in the lower left corner, abutting the Castle walls. The beginning of industrial development can also be seen along West Quay Road, in the distance. The Pirelli works closed in 1992. *A117273*

Arundel Towers, the former Hampshire County Council offices, demolished in 1997 to make way for the West Quay shopping centre. They spanned a site between Western Esplanade and Portland Terrace. The original Arundel Tower was part of the town walls and was named after Sir John Arundel who was appointed Governor of Southampton Castle in 1377.

Above Bar

THIS area of the city, from the Bargate, north to the bottom of the Avenue, was outside the medieval walled town and began its development largely during the eighteenth century.

The early part of that century saw Southampton in a state of industrial and commercial decline, as trade was lured away by other developing south coast ports. The writer Daniel Defoe thought the place was 'dying with age; the decay of the trade is the real decay of the town.' However, from the 1720's onwards the increasingly fashionable medicinal habit of taking the waters, coupled with the discovery of a mineral spring in the area North of the Bargate, gave Southampton a unique dual attraction to the visitor, who could also indulge in the practice of sea bathing. 'Cold bathing' was prescribed as a cure for an enormous variety of illnesses, from rheumatism to blood disorders, whilst the waters from the Chalybeate spring were reputed to have been especially effective in the cure of mad dog bites. Under the patronage of Frederick, Prince of Wales, and later of his three sons, the Dukes of York, Cumberland and Gloucester, the town quickly became an exclusive 'spa resort'. In the wake of royal favour lesser 'gentry and nobility' were attracted to the town, both for the summer season and to take advantage of the 'salubrious airs' on a more permanent basis.

This influx into the town led to reports of a scarcity of lodgings and much speculative building was swiftly undertaken to accommodate the well-heeled visitors and their demands. Although sea bathing and other associated activities were undertaken largely along the shore, especially at Mr Martin's Long Rooms, other amusements became concentrated further to the north of the town. Shops, coffee houses, hotels, circulating libraries and a theatre all developed in Above Bar, where elegant Georgian frontages and bow windows replaced narrow, timbered buildings and pushed the boundary of the urban town ever northwards.

Probably the most prestigious development was the Polygon. Envisaged as Southampton's equivalent to Bath's Royal Crescent, it was begun in 1768. Designed by the London architect, Jacob Leroux, it was to be a twelve-sided, twenty-two acre development comprising gentlemen's villas, an hotel, assembly rooms, card rooms and a tavern. Unfortunately only the hotel and three of the houses were completed before one of the investors went bankrupt and the others lost interest in the project. Although the hotel opened for the 1773 season, business was slow and social competition was stiff, especially from Martin's Long Rooms. The fate of the development was finally sealed by an incident at the masquerade ball in September, when a large stone was thrown through a window, narrowly missing the Duchess of Gloucester. There is still a Polygon Hotel on the site, although it is not the original building; two of the original houses can still be found amongst the later Victorian additions.

Development in Above Bar continued with the building of elegant Regency terraces such as Rockstone Place and Carlton Crescent, designed by the local architect, Samuel Edward Toomer, to provide suitable town houses for the 'season'. Carlton Crescent even included mews and a riding school, which was still described by Philip Brannon almost half a century later as 'in every respect the finest building in the kingdom devoted to this purpose'. It had cost £3,000, and throughout the summer a riding master gave instruction

The northern face of the Bargate, looking into Pembroke Square. The two lions were presented by William Lee in 1774 when he was made a burgess of the town. As can be seen from the nearer lamp, the photographer was standing in the George Yard where the town's fire engine was kept.

and public performances of equestrian techniques. The Thorner Charity Buildings were erected in 1794 on the site of what was to become Above Bar and Civic Centre Road, and building continued towards the Polygon with the magnificent Cumberland Place and Brunswick Place, recalling the town's royal associations.

As Southampton reached its peak of popularity as a spa resort, a number of estates and 'country seats' were established just outside the town to take advantage of the fine and still open views of the river and Southampton Water. Bellevue was built in 1768 at the bottom of the Avenue, by Nathaniel St Andre, the court physician to George I, and Archers Lodge and Bannisters Court were both built during the 1790s.

Although bathing remained a popular amusement in the town, Southampton began to wane as a 'spa resort' during the second decade of the nineteenth century. Her commercial position was not regained until the 1840s, with the coming of the railway and the new docks. In this period the town continued to attract visitors as well as witnessing a significant increase in population.

The commercial focus of the town expanded so Above Bar became as important as Below Bar, although it was never as intensely developed because the areas of common or Lammas land, which were declared public parks in 1844, could not be built upon.

Some important public buildings such as the offices of the Royal Ordnance were located in the Above Bar area, and businesses in the London Road thrived, serving the communities of the Regency terraces.

The real importance of the area began to take shape when the Town Council applied for an Act of Parliament to build a new Civic Centre on part of West Marlands in 1924. Opposition from notable citizens like William Burrough Hill, who claimed that the new town hall would be built in an 'obscure hole', coupled with the difficult passage of the bill though Parliament, meant that it was July 1930 before the foundation stone was laid by Prince Albert, the Duke of York, and building work really got underway. The design, by E.

Berry Webber, had been selected from 47 submitted in an open competition, and was to comprise four blocks, erected as separate contracts, but inter-connected to form a true Civic Centre.

The Municipal Offices were opened in November 1932, and the fourth and final block, consisting of the Art Gallery and Art School, was completed in 1936. Unfortunately, it was this part of the building which received a direct hit during a bombing raid on 6 November 1940, which resulted in the deaths of eighteen tutors and students of the Art School. (Civic employees).

The new Civic Centre, despite being described as a 'great white elephant' on a number of occasions, did succeed in determining the new municipal focus of the town as Above Bar.

The greatest change in the character of the area occurred during World War Two, when the importance of the docks and other works such as Supermarine and Pirelli made Southampton an obvious target for German bombs. Raids were not restricted to industrial targets and during November and December 1940, shops, cinemas, churches, schools, the Civic Centre and the Central Station were all repeatedly attacked.

The shortage of labour and materials in the immediate post-war years, together with the demands of a vital housing programme, led to delays in the reconstruction of the commercial centre of the city. However, after the rubble had been cleared, a large number of flat-roofed, single- and sometimes double-storey, temporary buildings did appear, in both Above and Below Bar, to house the many shops and businesses needing new premises.

Gradually throughout the 1950s and 1960s these were replaced. Tyrrell and Green's present building, designed by Yorke, Rosenberg and Mardell, opened in 1958, and Plummers and C&A constructed two multi-storey department stores on the Guildhall Square site. Despite ambitious post-war town planning, many of the new Above Bar buildings were criticised as ugly, commonplace or lacking in foresight, and many were certainly a stark contrast with what had gone before.

Southampton had an unique design of tram with small diameter wheels and a domed top to allow the vehicles to pass through the central arch of the Bargate. Fifty-one trams of this design were built at the Portswood tram depot from 1923 onwards. The demolition of the walls flanking the Bargate in 1932 and 1938 eliminated the need for such a specialised vehicle. *LSH 224*

Tramcar number nine outside the Bargate on 31 December 1949. It was the last tram to run in the city. Special last day tickets were issued and in the evening the tramcar was decorated with a blaze of coloured light bulbs. The following day all routes were replaced with diesel buses.

Shops on the east side of the Bargate, 1931-32, prior to the commencement of work on the Bargate Improvement Scheme. All of these buildings were demolished.

Aerial view of the city showing the post-war reconstruction of the High Street and Above Bar area. *54/943*

Pembroke Square, just east of the Bargate, after a heavy snowfall in April, 1905. Mr. Kimber, proprietor of the Pembroke Hotel, surveys the scene. *LSH1144*

The *Southampton Times and Hampshire Express* newspaper offices situated at 70 Above Bar. It was a weekly publication appearing on a Saturday and at the time of this picture, around 1916-17, was published by Charles Cox. There are several interesting advertisements in the office window appealing for 'strong girls' to undertake war work in the bookbinding and machine rooms. *M 6318*

The *Southern Echo* at 52 Above Bar, was the town's established daily paper. Costing ½d, the paper declared that 'besides giving prompt and full report of all matters of interest arising in the district' it also devoted 'special attention to cricket, football and sporting matters'. The *Independent* was a weekly publication which listed among its special features during the 1890s 'ladies tea time gossip'. *M 5859*

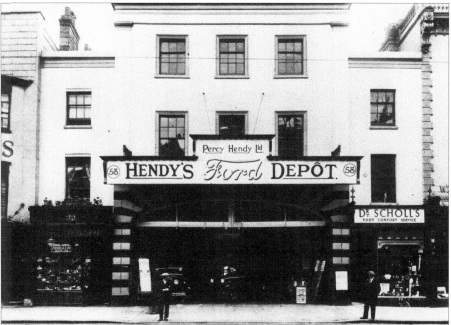

Hendy's Garage at 58 Above Bar around 1930. The company had given up manufacturing its own vehicles after a few years and taken on a Ford franchise which the company still holds today. Hendy's moved to nearby Vincernt's Walk after the Blitz and the site was later developed by Marks and Spencer, though redeveloped again at the end of the 20th. Century.

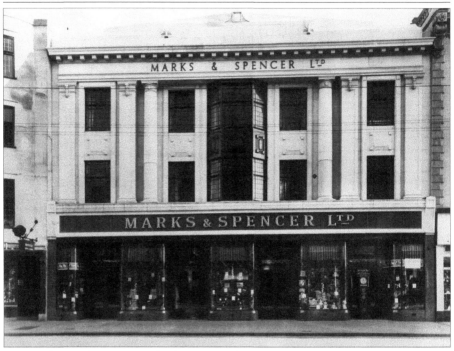

Marks and Spencer's opened their first 'Penny Bazaar' shop in East Street in 1906. By 1937, when this picture was taken, the business had grown considerably and the shop had relocated to 56-60 Above Bar Street. *M 5117*

Post-war rebuilding of the Above Bar area of the town, about 1950. The temporary wooden signposts are still in place.

The antiques business of William Borough Hill at the relatively short-lived site at 179 High Street, probably in 1920. At the beginning of the 20th. Century his premises were at 10 Above Bar and he later moved to Hanover Buildings.

Cumberland Place in the late 1970s after wartime bomb damage had destroyed the original elegant Georgian terrace. *54/1169*

Southampton School of Art and the Philharmonic Hall in Above Bar, located next to Scullard's Hotel. The building later became the Alexandra Picture House and the site was developed in the early 1930s to make way for the Regal Cinema which later became the Odeon, and is itself now demolished. The School of Art moved to premises in the new Civic Centre. The Philharmonic Hall was known for the quality of its concerts and summer lectures. Paganini once played there. *M5851.*

The Royal Hotel in Cumberland Place, later rebuilt as Southampton Park Hotel.

Above Bar Congregational Church. This was the third Congregational building on this site, the first being built in 1662. Isaac Watts the author and hymn writer was among those who worshiped here. The building illustrated was destroyed by enemy action in 1940.

An Above Bar Congregational Church Sunday School parade, around 1910. Both Church and Sunday School attendances were still high, and children were given incentives such as attendance medals and books to try to ensure that they continued their 'moral' education. *M 4466*

A new branch of the
National Provincial Bank,
now the National
Westminster Bank, being
built in Above Bar in 1932.
An interesting feature of
this photograph is the
wooden scaffolding. *PB3*

Above Bar with
considerable traffic
congestion and decorations
for the Silver Jubilee
Celebrations of George V,
May 1935.
*F.G.Bealing Collection. M
9672*

"The Junction" or Prospect Place, where Commercial Road meets Above Bar Street, with decorations for the Silver Jubilee of King George V on 8th. May, 1935. *M9673*

The soft furnishing department of Plummer Roddis' Shop on the corner of Prospect Place and Commercial Road, in the 1930s. The department store was a family business for 100 years. Despite the devastation caused by German bombs new premises were built on the same site, but the business finally closed its doors in 1993.

These houses in West Marlands were built in 1787 as Thorner's Charity almshouses for women and were demolished in 1930 to make way for the building of Civic Centre Road. Robert Thorner (1622 – 1709) who founded the charity, was an elder of Above Bar Independent Church.

The Receiving and Enquiry Office of the London and South Western Railway Company in Marland Place. The Southampton Art Society held their meetings on the upper floor.

The laying of the foundation stone of the Civic Centre, by Prince Albert, Duke of York, on 1 July 1930. The mayor at the time was Hector Young.

The Civic Centre, 31 May 1933. This dramatic building was the inspiration of Alderman Sir Sidney Kimber and the design was eventually chosen from 47 submitted in an open architectural competition in 1929. The addition of a tower to the planned design was made following an experiment by Kimber and Berry Webber, who tethered a balloon on the site at the height of the top of the proposed tower, and then drove around the town 'spotting' the balloon from various vantage points. *M 9668*

The original Art Gallery entrance shortly after completion of the Civic Centre in 1936.

The clock tower, now at Bitterne Park Triangle, was originally situated on the corner of Above Bar Street and New Road, but had to be moved in 1934 as part of a road improvement scheme. First erected in 1889 as a bequest from Mrs Henrietta Sayers, it incorporated a drinking fountain as well as a water trough for dogs. The clock is of German manufacture.

One of the elegant Regency terraces in Grosvenor Square was briefly used as a nursing home in the early years of this century. *M 4529*

Prospect Place about 100 years ago. The castellated building on the left, known as 'Ellyet's Folly' was the home of a Portsmouth businessman. It stood at the junction of Above Bar and Commercial Road, but was demolished shortly after the turn of the century to make room for more shops in the Above Bar area.

54/1259

Sussex Place, on the west side of Above Bar, in the mid 1890s. Debenham and Smith at number 1 was a photographic business and Willwam Dale's at number 5, was a piano warehouse.

Elegant Regency houses on the north side of Carlton Crescent. This area of Above Bar was developed during the Georgian period. Royal patronage of the town encouraged a number of 'men of rank and nobility' to take houses in the town during the season. *LSH 754*

The prestigious Polygon development, begun in 1768, was to be Southampton's answer to the Royal Crescent in Bath. Only three of the planned twelve houses, and the hotel, were actually constructed. The last house was replaced with a block of flats in 1999.

Rockstone Place – built by Samuel Edward Toomer, a local architect. between 1833-41. General Gordon of Khartoum lived here, – his parents having purchased No.5 in 1857. *M 2442*

Elegant Regency houses in Cumberland Place, overlooking Watts Park. *54/812*

Hurst Leigh School was a converted house in the Polygon, between Cumberland Place and Newcombe Road, next to the cricket ground. It catered for both boys and girls although they were strictly segregated. It was run by Mr and Mrs Caulifield from 1912 until 1935. *M10620*

Inside Hurst Leigh School. *M10623*

The auction rooms of William Borrough Hill in Carlton Place. *M6328*

The new Riding School at Carlton Place. This magnificent building managed to escape damage during the war and survives today as business premises.

London Road, pre-World War Two, showing St Paul's Church and 'domed' tramcar.

Grand Regency town houses situated in Anglesea Place, approximately on the site later occupied by C. & A. Modes at 133 Above Bar Street. By the early part of the 20th. century they had been converted to business premises to accommodate a solicitor, a dental surgeon and an insurance company. *54/1395*

London Road undergoing post-war rebuilding around 1950. The tramlines have been removed and the only surviving building of any age is the National and Provincial Bank on the corner of Carlton Crescent.

The imposing entrance of the Ordnance Survey building around 1880. The survey first came to Southampton as the result of a fire which destroyed the Map Office in the Tower of London in 1841. *TH 10/17*

The Royal Ordnance Building at the top of London Road, bedecked with flags for the Coronation of George VI in 1937. Built as cavalry barracks in the late eighteenth century it was subsequently used as a Royal Military Asylum for the orphans of soldiers before being turned over to the Royal Engineers of the Ordnance Survey in 1841. *F.G.Bealing Collection. M9674*

The Royal Engineers and enrolled pensioners of the Ordnance Survey, outside the Survey's Photographic Building during the 1880s. *Photograph courtesy of the Royal Engineers Museum. TH 10/17*

The Photographic Building of the Ordnance Survey Office. Early photographs enabled the Royal Engineers to produce some highly detailed maps of the mid-Victorian town, and during World War One the Southampton office produced 32 million maps including large numbers of trench maps. *Photograph courtesy of the Royal Engineers Museum. TH 10/17*

Interior of the Ordnance Survey Photographic Building. *Photograph courtesy of the Royal Engineers Museum. TH 10/17*

The Ordnance Survey Meteorological Observatory. *Photograph courtesy of the Royal Engineers Museum. TH 10/17*

Open Spaces

T HE public parks and open spaces within Southampton are probably the most prominent surviving features of the town's Victorian legacy. They all have their origins in medieval common land or Lammas lands. Such lands were owned by the hereditary burgesses of the town from Candlemas on 2 February until Lammas Day on 1 August. During this time they were fenced and cultivated, but the harvest had to be gathered by the end of the stipulated period, before the land reverted to common pasture for the remainder of the year. Philip Brannon, the local architect and artist, writing in 1850, noted 'That on more than one occasion when the summer proprietor has not removed his crops in time, the turn of noon of quarter day has seen such a rush of the poor, young and old, provided with fire irons, sticks, baskets, old kettles or whatever other implements could be adapted to the digging and removal of the booty.'

It was the passing of the Marsh Act in 1844 which secured the alteration for these lands from 'common lands' to public parks. The threat of disease and overcrowding in older parts of the town united factions of the Corporation in a determination to see the 'lungs' of Southampton preserved for the health and recreation of its people. The act enabled the Corporation to sell some of the marshlands as building plots, the proceeds being used to buy out the Lammas land interests in East and West Marlands (or St Magdalene's Lands), Highlands and Handwheel so that they could be established as public open space.

A second parliamentary act in 1865 confirmed the situation and stated that these areas be 'for ever devoted and kept exclusively as parks, gardens, pleasure grounds, play grounds and open spaces for the general and public advantage of the inhabitants of Southampton.'

However, it took almost 20 years for most of the parks to be formally laid out. West Park or Watts Park was only just planted when Isaac Watts' memorial statue was unveiled in 1861, and it was not until 1862 that the avenue of trees crossing Andrew's Park and Palmerston Park was presented to the town by the mayor, Frederick Perkins. Brannon's proposals for a botanic garden on the Marlands site never reached fruition.

Above Bar the main thoroughfare to London known as the Avenue, was laid out as early as 1745 by the Corporation of the town, under the mayoralty of Arthur Atherley. It is thought that many more of the magnificent trees were planted in the following year in commemoration of the battle of Culloden.

Unfortunately by the mid-nineteenth century, tree beetles and disease had attacked many of the elms, and the town council undertook a major replanting programme during the 1860s. However, an 1896 guide to the town suggested that the beauty of the Avenue was by no means spoiled, comparing its importance to the town with that of the Champs Elysees to the city of Paris.

The Avenue runs through the 376 acres of land known as 'The Common', (which first became common land during the thirteenth century, when a dispute over land rights between Nicholas de Sirlie, Lord of the Manor of Shirley, and the Burgesses of the town was terminated by the purchase of de Sirlie's rights by the Borough). It too became a public park in 1844, and was again described by Philip Brannon in 1850 as 'The finest piece of parkland belonging to any town in the Kingdom, blending the lawn and the grove, the open heath and sheltered glade, the graceful clump and the untrimmed wilderness'. Like the rest of Southampton's parks it had its origins in common grazing land, this usually being considered the most important of the rights of common, although every town household paying 'watch and ward' was also entitled to gather fuel, take clay for bricks and gather nuts, berries, rushes and any other wild produce.

The town cowherd, together with eight drivers, was the paid official responsible for the cattle on the common. He was provided with accommodation on the site of the present 'Cowherds' pub, which had become an inn during the 1760s following the replacement of the original fifteenth-century cottage under the patronage of a town alderman called Knight. He subsequently raised the rent to such an extent that it could only be found by using the new house as an inn. The town council then let the property to a local firm of brewers, Taylor, Moody and Taylor, who still reserved accommodation for the cowherd.

Another town official who lived and worked on the common was the town brickmaker, who also assisted the cowherd in maintaining the fences and hedges. This seems to have become a family business under the Hardens of Toothill but when William Harden went bankrupt in 1814, the lease on his property was purchased by the town clerk, who demolished the original house and erected a 'gentleman's villa', known as Hawthorn Cottage. Later owned by the local shipbuilder John Ransom, it was virtually derelict by 1945 when the council bought back the lease and re-leased the site to the Chipperfield circus family for use as a 'zoological pets corner'.

Until the seventeenth century Southampton 's annual Court Leet was held on the common. This ancient Anglo Saxon law court enabled freemen of the town to meet in order to punish petty criminals or to resolve local disputes. Last held on the mound known as Cutthorn in 1670, Southampton was able to preserve this ancient tradition, and is today one of only three towns able to hold a Court Leet. The Court still meets annually on the first Tuesday after Michaelmas, but is now presided over by the Sheriff in the relative comfort of the Civic Centre.

Despite the prevalence of highwaymen on the common during the eighteenth century, it was inevitable that such a large expanse of attractive open land should be used for leisure purposes, especially as the population increased and the fashionable nobility and gentry were attracted to the town as a spa resort. A carriage drive was laid out, followed by a racecourse in 1822. The four man-made lakes which had originally supplied water to the town were gradually turned over to ornamental or boating purposes and the model yacht club are recorded using the pool near the 'Cowherd' as early as 1894. Cricket, football and golf were all played on the common after its conversion to public park status, and before more permanent venues were established. As the town's population expanded and building developments reduced the number of suitable large sites in the centre of the town, the common became a popular ground for shows, fairs and circuses. The Royal Counties Agricultural Show was a regular feature throughout the 1920s and the Southampton Horticultural Show grew out of a wartime 'dig for Victory' garden fête. An annual show with a gardening theme has continued in the summer, but its popularity in recent years is much diminished.

Southampton's military role as a major port of embarkation for troops travelling overseas has meant that the Common, has been used as military billets. It is probable that soldiers fighting in the Hundred Years War and the Napoleonic Wars camped there, although during the nineteenth century it was largely used for training exercises by local regiments. World War One and Two saw far more intensive occupation, by prisoners of war as well as soldiers. After the war the army were slow to vacate the common, and with a desperate housing shortage in the City many of the huts were taken over by squatters. One area known as 'Squatters Camp' was actually run by the council's Housing Department and the Ministry of Housing for some years; it even had an official camp commandant. Finally returned to public ownership, the last hut was not demolished until 1953.

Today, Southampton's parks and open spaces are still protected under the act that established them in 1849, and remain an attractive and important leisure facility in the heart of the busy modern city.

Aerial View of Mayflower Park looking back towards the City, where a large expanse of the ancient walls can be seen: a view now obscured by more recent building.

Dancing at the open air swimming pool known as The Lido, on Western Esplanade during the 1930s. It was a popular social venue for all age groups, but finally closed in the 1970s when it was replaced by a new indoor pool.

A view across Queen's Park to Queen's Terrace around 1900. Queen's Park, situated behind the Platform and looking north towards Oriental Terrace around 1900. There were many hotels in this area which were especially popular with yachting parties during the summer, the park providing an excellent view of the waterfront. The memorial is to General Gordon of Khartoum and dates from 1885.

Cast iron gas column erected by public subscription in 1822 to commemorate the gift of street lights by William Chamberlayne. Originally at the corner of Northam Bridge Road and Above Bar, it was moved to Town Quay in 1829 to act as a navigation beacon. It was photographed in 1945 on the roundabout outside Hoglands Park, and was moved several yards in 1957 on the creation of Queensway. Having been refurbished, it has resided at the south end of Houndwell Park since 2000.

Major Dalton Newfield of the US Army, with three military police, standing at the entrance to Hoglands Park. The park became the headquarters of the US 14th Major Port during the build up to D-Day.

The unveiling ceremony of the Ransom drinking fountain on Asylum Green in 1866. John Ransom, standing immediately to the left of the fountain, was a prominent Victorian shipbuilder who claimed to own the largest fleet of wooden vessels in the port during the 1860s. The fountain was designed by the architect and borough surveyor, George Poole.

Viscount Palmerston of Broadlands, Romsey was a burgess of Southampton. Following his death in 1865 a commemorative statue was commissioned from Thomas Sharp of London and unveiled in 1869. The park, previously called Fair Field was renamed Palmerston Park.

The Southampton War Memorial on the edge of West Park in 1952. It was designed by Sir Edwin Lutyens and was a prototype for his London Cenotaph.

East Park Terrace overlooking East Park, from which this photograph was taken in 1895. *M6273*

The Isaac Watts Memorial in Watts Park, overlooking Cumberland Place, The statue was unveiled by the Earl of Shaftesbury on 17 July 1861, Watts' birthday.

The *Titanic* engineers' memorial on the edge of East Park. Unveiled on 22 April 1914, it commemorates the engineers, most of whom were local men, who lost their lives when the 'unsinkable' ship hit an iceberg in mid Atlantic on 15 April 1912.

The ornate Victorian memorial to Richard Andrews in East Park. Unfortunately, the Bath Stone used for the elaborate pedestal failed to resist the effects of weathering and it was removed in 1971, a century after its erection. The figure of Andrews still remains in the park but now on a much smaller and less splendid plinth.

Stag Gates, in a photograph taken some time pre-1905. This early Victorian gateway marked the entrance to the former estate of Bevois Mount House, and stood where Lodge Road meets The Avenue. They were demolished as a 'risk to traffic' shortly after being presented to the city in 1919. *M5806*

The area at the north-east of the Common known as 'Cutthorn' showing the board giving details of Courts Leet held there from Anglo-Saxon times. The ceremony now takes place in the Civic Centre on the first Thursday in October each year 'Cutthorn' may refer to the ancient method of making cuts on trees to denote boundaries.

A view of the Inner Avenue around 1900.

The Avenue, drawn and engraved by Philip Brannon. This renowned entrance to the Town, across the Common, was originally planted by the Town Corporation in 1745, more trees being planted the following year in commemoration of the Battle of Culloden. Sadly many of these were destroyed by boring beetle and the town council was forced to undertake an extensive replanting programme in the 1860s. *54/1108*

Mr Tom Barrow and his horse, Tom, at the Southampton Show held on the Common in the early 1960s. Mr Barrow was one of the last Southampton Corporation roadsweepers to work with a horse and cart.

The pub now known as 'The Cowherd' has also been known as 'The Southampton Arms', and prior to that was actually the home of the town cowherd. There was a cottage close by called 'The Hawthorns', hence the name of the Natural History Study Centre operated by the City Council nearby. *54/621*

The common was used as a venue for all kinds of entertainment including horse racing, fairs, pageants and circus shows. *54/2140*

"Cemetery Lake" towards the north of the Common was popular for rowing, especially when the fair was being held nearby.

During the 1850s when this engraving was
produced, Regent's Park was still a rural area on
the edge of the town. Popular for promenading
and carriage rides, the road wound its way
through several 'country' estates. *54/1117*

Frank Cox of Southampton First Troup
known as the "First All Saints", at a summer
camp on the Common in 1914. He joined the
Scouts in 1913. *LSH527*

By the 1890s Regents Park had become
incorporated into the district of Shirley.
Although more private residences were built
it retained its 'rural' image until major
suburban development got under way in the
1920s and '30s.

The Waterfront

T HE value of the Southampton area as a port, due to its sheltered position and prolonged high tide, has been recognised since the Isle of Wight became separated from the mainland five thousand years ago. In spite of these benefits, sailing ships had to be beached in order to take on or unload cargo, or had to anchor off shore and have the goods transferred to smaller craft for transfer on to the quays.

Civic involvement with port activities may be traced to 1451, when King Henry VI bestowed the honorary title of 'Admiral of the Port' on the mayor. Many years later, in 1803, the Corporation established the Harbour Commissioners to regulate traffic. Originally the town walls were almost at the water's edge, but beyond the walls were West Quay, to which access was gained via the West Gate, and what is now Town Quay, reached by way of the Water Gate, now demolished. The commissioners extended Town Quay, built warehouses, and constructed a pier for steam packets plying to France, the Channel Islands and the Isle of Wight. This was opened in 1833 by Her Royal Highness Princess Victoria (later Queen Victoria).

The Harbour Commissioners evolved into the Harbour Board in 1863, with statutory duties regarding the port, but the resources of the local authority could not stretch to the construction of the more elaborate docks which were needed for the repair and maintenance of ships, as well as for their accommodation. Private enterprise was allowed to take advantage of this opportunity, and the first development, the Open Dock, built on mud land to the east of Town Quay, was opened by the Southampton Dock Company in 1842, the foundation stone having been laid in 1838 by Sir Lucius Curtis. *Tagus* and *Liverpool* of the Peninsular and Oriental Steamship Company were the first vessels to use it.

The Close Dock or Inner Dock leading off what then became the Outer Dock, was opened in 1851, but these facilities soon proved unable to cope with the increasing size and number of ships using the port. This situation led to the construction of the Empress Dock, which was opened in 1890. This made Southampton the only port in Britain which could allow the movement of the world's largest ships at all states of the tide.

The resources of the Southampton Dock Company were always under strain, and their financial indebtedness to the London and South Western Railway lead to their eventual takeover by the railway company in 1892.

The White Star Line first came to Southampton in 1907 with their *Adriatic*, then the largest ship in the world, but it was clear that the growing size of transatlantic vessels would require still larger docks: as a result Ocean Dock was opened in 1911. Its associated dry dock, Trafalgar Dry Dock, which opened in 1905, was even bigger than the Prince of Wales Dry Dock of 1895. However, the size of vessels and volume of traffic continued to increase.

Pressure for space had caused the London and South Western Railway to order a floating dry dock for the then largest liners. This was not delivered until after the railway grouping, by which time the dock's new owners, the Southern Railway, had put in hand a scheme to construct a New Docks with two miles of deep-water quay. Later a vast dry dock, the King George V Graving Dock, was built at its western edge, designed specifically to accommodate ships of the size of *Queen Mary*. This new dock estate was sufficiently complete to receive its first ship, the Cunard *Mauritania*, in 1932.

The New Docks later became known as the Western Docks to distinguish them from the existing Eastern Docks.

Imperial Airways established their Empire Air Base for flying boats in the Western Docks in 1937; this transferred to a specially constructed jetty in the Eastern Docks after World War Two.

In 1968, the docks, now in the ownership of the British Transport Docks Board, were further extended to the west of King George V dry dock, to form a specialised container terminal. The Inner Dock, having been redundant for some time, was filled in, and the Outer Dock became, with modifications, the Princess Alexandra Dock – primarily a ferry terminal with connections to Bilbao and Le Havre.

Following dock privatisation, Associated British Ports took over operations in Southampton in 1983, and this heralded further changes in the size and use of the waterfront. Developments along the River Test have doubled the length of quayside of the original Western Docks. The container terminal mentioned above has been adapted for the import and export of vehicles, in which Southampton plays a very big part; and the Prince Charles Container Terminal has been established, making Southampton the second largest container port in the country. At the same time, areas of the original docks have become redundant because they could not be adapted to modern requirements. These have been skilfully reused for leisure pursuits with the establishment of Ocean Village in the area of the old Outer and Inner Docks, and the redevelopment of Town Quay.

The railway conceived of as the London and Southampton Railway in 1834 became fully operational as the London and South Western Railway in 1840, with an impressive terminus, designed by Sir William Tite, just inland from the new Open Dock. Construction of the Southampton and Dorchester Railway was authorised in 1845 and linked with the existing line by means of a tunnel under the town: the company amalgamated with the London and South Western Railway soon after, in 1848. This second line brought Southampton West or Blechynden Station into use, which, with various name changes, has become the main railway station, Southampton Terminus Station having closed in 1966.

The entrance building to the Docks Station in Terminus Terrace, designed by Sir William Tite. The presence of overhead wires date this as after the electrification of the tramway in 1901. It was renamed Southampton Terminus Station by the Southern Railway in July 1923.

A picture painted in the 1850s, of what was then called Southampton Docks Station, with Tite's imposing building on the right, the covered train shed in the centre, and the engine shed which existed then, on the left. Some of the original locomotives of the LSWR were built locally by Day, Summers.

A photograph taken from the top of the South Western Hotel, looking north, with the LSWR goods shed, completed in the late 1880s, on the right, Central Bridge, opened in 1882 to replace busy level crossing, appropriately in the centre; and the parcels office and cattle dock on the left. *M6010*

South Western Hotel at the corner of Terminus Terrace and Canute Road. Built in 1867 as the Imperial Hotel, it was taken over by the London and South Western Railway in 1882, then enlarged in the 1920s. It was requisitioned by the Navy in 1940, and has never reverted to being a hotel. *54/45*

The first railway line across Canute Road was in place for the opening of the docks in 1842, and a second line was added in the 1850s. The large building in the centre, the LSWR Maritime Chambers, was not built until 1899.

The Southern Railway Continental Booking Office at the Outer Dock, still survives as part of the frontage of Canutes Pavilion at the heart of the Ocean Village leisure complex, Railway steamers departed for the Channel Islands and French ports. A good example of a hydraulic crane is visible in the background. Water under pressure was used originally for powering cranes, capstans and the lock gates.

Lloyd's Bank near Dock Gate 7 in Canute Road in the early 1920s prior to its extension. Note the taxi outside.

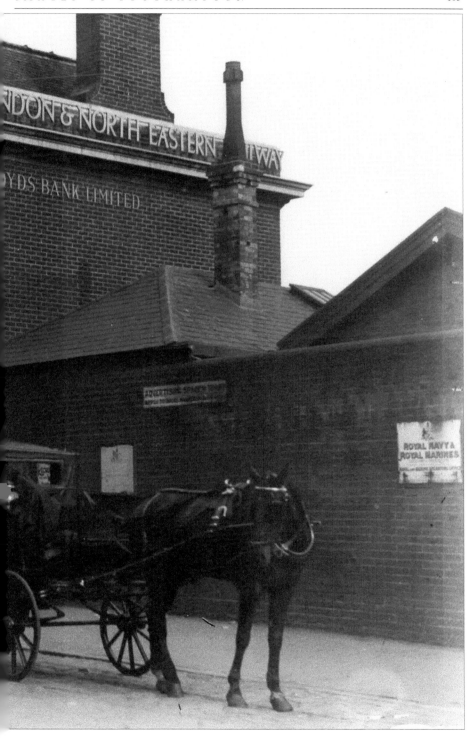

An unusual subject for the camera, but one which must have been performed repeatedly, the bunkering of a ship from a barge, in this case the Southern Railway steamer Haslemere.

The Alexandra Towing Company came to Southampton just after World War One. This is their 700 ton tender Flying Kestrel, built by J.T.Eltingham of South Shields in 1913, their third vessel of that name. She was photographed before she went north to assist in the launch of the Queen Mary, at the grain warehouse, berth 18, the Inner Dock.

Empress Dock was opened by Queen Victoria on 26 July, 1890, adding 3,800 feet of quay frontage to the existing docks. The entrance to No.5, (Prince of Wales) dry Dock is just visible on the extreme left. This picture was taken just after World War One and shows a Royal Mail and a Union Castle ship.
32

The Empress Dock as depicted in a Ridgways advertisement. *Kildonan Castle* was the last steamer built for the Castle Line in 1899, before amalgamation with the Union Steam Ship Co.

Extending south of Empress Dock, is a peninsula with quays on the Itchen (right-hand) side and Test side. The empty Prince of Wales Dry Dock, opened in 1895, can be seen on the right, and near the centre is the International Cold Storage and Ice Company building. When bombed in 1940, it contained much of the Nation's butter supplies and as a consequence, burned for several days.

Construction of the Ocean Dock for White Star Line. The black and white funnels of an American line vessel can be seen in the adjacent Empress Dock.

White Star liner Olympic in the floating dry dock in May 1934. This dry dock ceased to be of major importance after the opening of King George V Dry Dock and it went to the Admiralty in Portsmouth in 1940. *ABP2280*

A site seen in various guises until the 1960s when the practice was outlawed. Messrs Andrews fuelling an imporEtd car at the docks from one of their mobile filling stations. Andrews, five times mayor of Southampton, was a coachbuilder, and one of the many skilled artisans who set up business here in the spa period.

Simons' Auction Rooms in the 1920s. French produce came to the docks from the Channel Islands, South Africa and elsewhere, and was auctioned on the spot.

An early feature of post-war reconstruction in Southampton, was the Ocean Terminal for passenger liners, at Ocean Dock. The prime minister, Clement Attlee is seen here having unveiled the commemorative plaque at its opening on 31 July 1950. It was an integrated passenger and baggage handling complex with its own rail platforms.

The seaward end of the 1,297 feet long Ocean Terminal building, with customs offices in the tower. Here the visitors' balcony is in full use and *Queen Elizabeth* is being refuelled along side.

The landward end of the Ocean Terminal building, with *Queen Mary* moored along side and a Pulman train in the foreground. The building was demolished in 1983.

One of the two Ocean Terminal departure lounges.

The joiners' shop of Harland & Wolff before World War One. Note the line shafting along the wall
with belts driving machines, and the electric arc light suspended from the ceiling. All woodworking
trades were housed under one roof with pattern making, cabinet making and French polishing a the
'upper' end. The buildings were remodelled and extended in 1917.

An empty but flooded Trafalgar Dry Dock behind the former Harland and Wolff ship repair shops. For a time, the facility was operated by Vosper, Thornycroft, as shown here.

The sailmakers' shop of Harland & Wolff in about 1910. Merchant ships often carried a full set of sails at this time, although the practice was fast declining.

The recently opened BOAC Flying Boat Terminal, photographed in June 1949. The jetty has two forked pontoons into which the hulls of the aircraft float. The terminal building later became HMS Wessex, headquarters of the Solent division of the RNR.

The old Outer Dock in its new guise as Princess Alexandra Dock for continental car ferries.

Geddes Warehouse with Seaway House, once the chamber of commerce, next door, looking east towards the dome-roofed Harbour Board Offices which were built in 1925 and contain paneling from the famous liner *Teutonic*.

The final meeting of Southampton Harbour Board on 25 July 1968.
(Donald S.Herbert).

A view from Town Quay looking towards the shore, c.1890. In this quiet scene, people are fishing from the Quay. Beyond them can be seen the Castle Hotel building at the foot of the High Street where the Water Gate stood until it was demolished in 1805 to make access to the Quay easier. The Castle Hotel building, lost during World War II, now reveals a portion of the town walls round which it was built. Further to the right are two more hotels. Lots of cheap accommodation was needed for seafarers and emigrants alike. *54/24*

These two pictures form a panorama of the harbour basin formed between Town Quay on the left and the Eastern Docks on the right. They were taken in the early 1930s by a talented amateur photographer, F.G.Bealing from the top of the wheelhouse of the White Star liner RMS *Majestic*. His vantage point was further raised because she was in the floating dry dock at the time. Many landmarks from other photographs in this book can be seen in context here.

The corner of French Street and Porters' Lane in about 1910. This building did not survive World War Two, but the building just visible on the right, Geddes or 'H' Warehouse, remains, now converted into flats.

The entrance to the Royal Pier photographed by F.G.Bealing in May 1937, and splendidly decorated to celebrate the Coronation of George VI. The ornamental lions on the roof have now lost their flags, but were transferred from the previous building on its demolition.

The Refreshment Rooms on the Royal Pier photographed in 1980, looking south, with the Pavilion just visible on the right. The pier was severely damaged by fire in 1988 and has never reverted to its former use.

The Pier Pavilion in its heyday.

Not a very clear view, but a rare one, taken from a Supermarine flying boat. The unusual feature of this picture is the presence, in the foreground, of an extra jetty to the west of the Pier. This was constructed in 1917 to handle the growing quantities of stores and supplies required by the forces, direct by rail from a junction at Southampton West, or Blechynden Station; the unusual craft also visible in the picture, is thus a train ferry. Operations ceased in 1919 and the structure was dismantled in the 1920s.

The magnificent headquarters of the Royal Southampton Yacht Club, built in 1846 at the foot of Bugle Street, with the pier master's house on the left. The present pier buildings are much further back from the road, which today leads to a busy roundabout.

This London and South Western Railway photograph is titled Storm Water Pipes, but our interest is in other features. It shows the site where Mayflower Park was constructed on reclaimed land in the early 1930s. Behind this and to the left, are two monuments. The smaller, a fountain, commemorates stewardess Mary Ann Rogers, who in 1899, gave her own life in a heroic effort to save passengers when the Stella was wrecked on the Casquet Rocks in the Channel Islands. The other commemorates the departure point of the Pilgrim Fathers in 1620, although they were forced to put in to Dartmouth and finally Plymouth before leaving the country. *36*

It was only in 1900 that Western Esplanade was opened up as a through route to the Royal Pier. Formerly there was no access round the outside of the walls past Westgate, shown here between the Royal Standard and a single-story building which was Madame Mae's Lodge.

The house known as Madame Mae's House, built against the walls, was demolished to form the connection, Madame Mae, a much travelled woman, had become the Margravine of Anspach in Germany, and left in 1812 although her name continued to be linked with the house.

A watercolour by David Law, of Pickett's Boat Yard, West Quay, in 1807.

In 1896, the Corporation bought the Southampton Electric Light and Power Company, and built a new generating station served by a siding from the railway line at the West Station, on what was then the Western Shore. It came into use in 1904 and appropriately, used electric shunting locomotives, using a single overhead wire in tram fashion.

The former coastline can clearly be seen in this 1930s view. The curve of the former bay bounded by Western Esplanade is towards the centre of the picture, with the High Street, the black line further to the right. Earlier evidence of encroachment into the water can be seen in the power station and the Pirelli factory. The need for docks can clearly be seen in the mud by the pier where a paddle steamer is stranded for the time being, and another has left her impression.

Two views of the Western Shore in the days before there was much encroachment into the water. One shows Weymouth Terrace which had a fine view, but was occasionally flooded on very high tides, and the other, the elevated Forest View, at the end of which are some of the country's first concrete houses. The bump in the road behind the audience effectively reduces the slope of Bargate Street.

Although only taken in September 1926, this panoramic view which shows the bay beyond the Town Walls just before it disappeared in the new dock development, looks much older. The Tudor Merchants' Hall, formerly the fish market in St Michael's Square, but moved here in 1634, is partially obscured by a tree.

The Western Docks when quite new, looking due east towards the original docks. These are berths 101 and 102, but a whole series of standard transit sheds was built with an integral rail network. The square piece of land jutting out at the end of the Western Docks is Mayflour Park, incorporated in the original development scheme as a substitute for the lost shoreline.

The Western Docks, berths 104 to 109, in 1970, occupied by *S.A. Vaal*, *Nevasa*, *Iberia*, *Orsova*, *Chusan*, and a cable ship. Here also can be seen the development of industry in the hinterland, the near units being the submarine cable factory of Standard Telephones and Cables Ltd, with the factory of A.C.Delco Ltd, further inland. Millbrook Station can just be seen in the top right.

Joseph Rank's Solent Flour Mills – the first and for a long time, only occupant of the industrial area created by the Western Docks, photographed here in the 1960s.

Vehicle import and export area in the foreground, with the developing Prince Charles Container Port behind.

Dry docks have long provided intrepid photographers with dramatic pictures. Here the White Star *Majestic* poses on the blocks in King George V Dock. She was already jointly owned by Cunard before the enforced merger of 1932 and started as the *Bismark*, being taken in war reparations after World War One. The objects in the foreground are paint barges.

God's House Tower, part of the ancient fortifications of Southampton, with a column of US troops approaching the celebrated bowling green during the build-up to D-Day in 1944. Even the Jeep is driving on the wrong side of the road.

In this post D-Day picture taken from the vantage point of the Yacht Club building opposite the pier, Axis troops taken prisoner in France are being marched from a landing craft to the prison compound in the New Docks.

The River Itchen

IN this chapter we deal with maritime activity on the river from its confluence with the Test, upstream to Northam Bridge, and the communities on both banks associated with this, namely Chapel, Northam, Itchen Ferry and Woolston.

The estuary of the River Itchen formed the municipal boundary of Southampton until 1920. Woolton, on the east bank, was an ancient hamlet, with Itchen Ferry, the eastern terminus of the steam-driven chain ferry inaugurated in 1836, forming a separate community. Rapid expansion followed the establishment of the Oswald, Mordaunt shipyard in 1860. This yard later belonged to Fay and Co, becoming John I.Thornycroft and Co in 1904 (now Vosper-Thornycroft).

Close to the shipyard, and further upstream the visionary aircraft designer Noel Pemberton-Billing started experimenting in 1908 and formed the Supermarine Aircraft Company in 1912. Supermarine was famous for its flying boats – aircraft with a fuselage like the hull of a ship and which use water as a runway. The factory was ideally situated for the construction of these craft, and attracted such remarkable people as Hubert Scott-Paine, world water-speed record holder and founder of Imperial Airways, and Reginald Mitchell, designer of the Spitfire. Supermarine also played a major role in both World Wars.

Another landmark in this area was the half-mile-long Rolling Mill at Weston just to the south of Woolston. This was developed by the Ministry of Munitions for the production of brass strip used to make small calibre shell cases. The rolling mill, which opened in 1917, was built partly on land which had been acquired by the London and South Western Railway for possible dock extension in 1908.

Woolston only became firmly cemented to Southampton in 1977 with the opening of the Itchen Bridge, replacing the chain ferry known as the Floating Bridge.

On the western bank of the Itchen, there were a few shipyards by the eighteenth century, mainly producing small naval craft. Most notable was the Northam Yard just below Northam Bridge (itself opened in 1796), and Chapel Yard, just up stream from the Crows House terminus of the Floating Bridge, these were both in rural surrounds. In about 1804, the Chapel Yard was converted into cargo wharves which later became the dominant feature.

Another significant industrial event occurred in Chapel in 1781 with the coming into use of the first steam engine in Southampton, this was at a factory producing ships biscuits for the Admiralty.

Two industrial railway lines, the Northam quay line and the Chapel Railway, were constructed in the 1840s, with a third, Bull's Run siding, added in the 1860s. Industrial development went hand in hand with these, with coke works, super phosphate works, saw mills, cement works, and between 1891 and 1960, a margarine factory, all contributing to the prosperity of the area. The gas works of the Southampton Gas Light and Coke Company, although opened in 1821, was not connected to the railway until 1873. Its gasholders, two of which remain today, have formed a landmark for many years.

Round these developments sprang up rows of terraced houses whose occupants have always had strong links with the sea. Of the total crew of 898 on board the *Titanic*, the majority came from Southampton and most of them lived in the areas of Chapel and Northam.

The character and use of the wharves has changed over the years, there is now no ship building or yacht building. Ship breaking,which followed, has also ceased, but ship repair continues. The movement of timber, coal, coke and chemicals has been replaced by the export of scrap, and the importation of sand, gravel and aggregate.

The River Itchen curves round from the bottom left to meet the Test running across the top of this picture, taken in about 1936. Northam Bridge is at the bottom, with the wharves of Northam and Chapel running towards the centre where the gas holders and retorts of the gasworks can be seen. The Rolling Mill at Weston can just be seen in line with the jetty at the mouth of the Itchen.

Cross House had bathing machines for a short time in the 1820s. Itchen Ferry was not only the name of the village on the opposite shore, but also the name of a type of vernacular craft used as a conveyance before the coming of the Floating Bridge. They were also used for fishing, but sadly the type is almost extinct today.

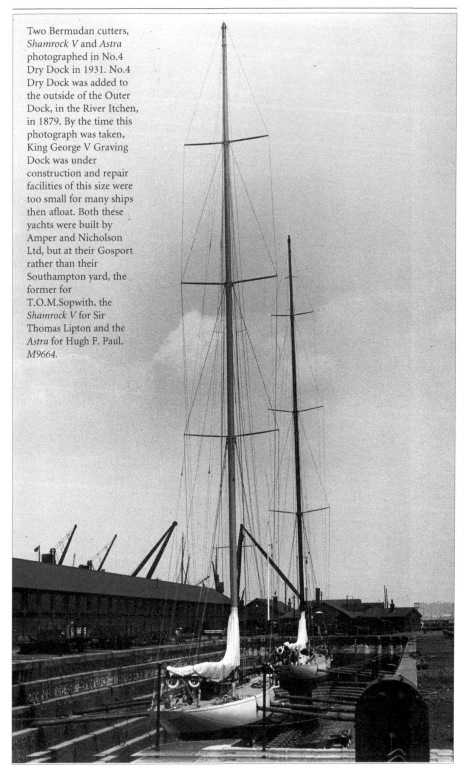

Two Bermudan cutters, *Shamrock V* and *Astra* photographed in No.4 Dry Dock in 1931. No.4 Dry Dock was added to the outside of the Outer Dock, in the River Itchen, in 1879. By the time this photograph was taken, King George V Graving Dock was under construction and repair facilities of this size were too small for many ships then afloat. Both these yachts were built by Amper and Nicholson Ltd, but at their Gosport rather than their Southampton yard, the former for T.O.M.Sopwith, the *Shamrock V* for Sir Thomas Lipton and the *Astra* for Hugh F. Paul. *M9664.*

The Floating Bridge across the Itchen was opened in 1836, and continued to operate until replaced by the present Itchen Bridge in 1977. Bridges after No.10 were diesel powered. The Floating Bridge allowed Woolston, a peaceful hamlet, to become home to many more affluent Sotonians who built villas there to escape from the town.

The western point of departure for the Floating Bridge, near Cross House, in the 1930s.

Floating Bridge No.3, built by Joseph Hodgkinson at Cross House in 1862. This is a carriage bridge as opposed to the small workers' bridges, that is horse-drawn vehicles could be accommodated in the central open space, with machinery and boilers down the sides and room for passengers by the railings on the extreme edges.

Floating Bridge No.9 arriving at the Southampton side. This one was built at Woolston in 1900 and retained the archaic beam engine of former craft of this type. The cables used to guide and allow it to pull itself along can clearly be seen.

A pen and wash drawing by an unknown artist, of Mr Roe's Wharf at Northam, about 1840.

Dock Street, Chapel, in 1929. This area was filled with a number of similar streets where many of the town's seamen and dockers lived.

Discharging coal from a railway wagon into a waiting barge at the Coal Barge Dock near Cross House, in 1920. The barge would then be towed alongside a ship to replenish its bunkers. The dock does not look busy. some steam ships were fired by oil in World War One, and this trend continued so that by the 1930s motor ships and oil-burning steam ships together accounted for half the merchant fleet.

Interior of Risdon, Beazley Marine Trading Company's new boat shed, 1934. *Warrior* in the centre, was a conversion of an Admiralty launch by the company into a twin-screw schooner, for Captain K.B.Harbord. During World War Two, Risdon, Beazley themselves built many launches for the Admiralty, to a standard American design.

Millbank Street, Northam, leading to Pollock Browns the ship breakers, in the 1950s. Television is beginning to make its appearance.

Pollock Brown & Co Ltd, took over the site of Northam Ironworks shown here in an aerial view, from shipbuilders Day, Summers, but engaged in ship breaking as well as undertaking steel fabricating and construction work. This view was taken in the 1930s.

The interior of Pollock Brown's steel fabricating shop in the 1920s. Many of their buildings were those of the previous occupants of the site, and this one, which has seen better days judging by the state of the roof, was originally Day, Summers' erecting shop of 1890.

A close up view of Pollock Brown's ship breaking activities in 1959, where the boiler of a bug, still well lagged with asbestos, is being removed in portions. Asbestos from South Africa was also a major import at this time. In the background is the tug-tender Paladin, on the slipway of the adjacent J.I. Thornycroft repair yard.

The first Northam Bridge opened in 1799. Unlike Cobden Bridge further up stream at St Denys, which was opened in 1883, there was a toll to pay to cross at Northam until 1929.

The Old Parsonage Itchen Ferry.

This magnificent panorama, taken from high ground on the east bank of the River Itchen, shows a relatively sparsely populated Woolston compared with the heavily built-up west bank. The series of photographs must have been taken in about 1870, for in view C, the Inner and Outer Docks are fully occupied, but no work has commenced on Empress Dock. While in view E, the railway from St Denys can be seen curving sharply round to Woolston Station, opened in 1866, which must be behind the camera. There is some distortion due to the movement of the camera, but view A shows Portsmouth Road running across the picture with the London Arms in the centre. In view B, Portsmouth Road descends to the Itchen Ferry which is obscured from view, and is met by Hazel Road and Laurel Road. In view C, there is a ferry just visible behind the buildings in the centre of the picture. Hazel Road itself disappears behind a hillock in view D, but the ferry can be seen on the other bank. If all the views were intended to overlap, then, unfortunately, there is one of the sequence missing, for in view E, we are looking across at Chapel from Sea Road.

Victoria Road, Woolston, in the 1940s.

Taken from the Woolston side of the Itchen, looking towards the timber importing wharves of chapel
with the spire of St Mary's Church in the background, this Supermarine *Sea Eagle* is depicted
preparing to take off on an endurance test flight.

Thornycroft's Jetty in the 1920s looks deserted, yet only a few years previously it had been a hive of activity, producing submarines and the well-known, modified 'M' class destroyers, with great rapidity. This yard in Woolston continues today as Vosper Thornycroft, and started in the 1860s as Oswald, Mordaunt's yard in which many famous sailing ships were built. Note the slipway with the 'Belfast' roof to shelter construction workers.

This archway which stood in Weston Lane marked one of the entrances to the Chamberlayne Estate at Weston Grove. It was demolished in the 1950s to allow buses to travel along the land and is now the site of Squires Walk, Weston.

This pillared arch was situated on Weston Lane and marked an entrance to the estate of Lord Radstock. It was demolished in the 1930s.

Supermarine Woolston works in
the late 1920s. In the centre of the
picture, new buildings, identifiable
by their light-coloured roofs, have
replaced the earliest structures
although Pemberton-Billing's
shipyard and slipway to the left has
yet to be developed. To the right,
one of the two operating floating
bridges can be seen, with the spare
bridge in its dock just next to the
Supermarine works.

Southampton's Suburbs

St Mary's

ST MARY'Ss is one of the oldest occupied suburbs in Southampton. It stands on the site of the Saxon town of Hamwic or Hamtun, which was an important international trading centre by the eighth century. Although the location of the town had moved west, inside the Norman walls, by the Middle Ages, and the original settlement was almost forgotten, the minster church of the Saxon town remained. St Mary's church, although re-built many times, still remains the Mother Church of Southampton.

The Saxon town was re-discovered largely in the mid-Victorian period when population pressure within the medieval, walled town encouraged developers to consider expansion into the fields and glebe lands surrounding the old church. Many of the discoveries were made during the extraction of brick earth from the fields to make the bricks for the new Victorian terraces. Although some finds were recorded and do survive, many of the workmen found it more profitable to sell the contents of the pits that they were excavating. it was estimated that 50 tons of ancient bones from the site were sold to local bone merchants in 1849.

With a population of 34,000 by 1851, two-thirds of whom were living in St Mary's Ward, housing became the primary consideration, and the 'modern' suburb of St Mary's began to take shape. In addition to domestic dwellings, a new gaol was built in 1855, to the south of Clifford Street and a new workhouse for the poor of the parish and a thriving market developed in Kingsland. Being so close to the town centre, much of St Mary's Victorian character was destroyed by German bombs during World War Two, and later by the new Six Dials road scheme, but the area still remains an important suburb supporting businesses, had market and a technical college.

St Mary's Church engraved by Philip Brannon in about 1850, looking rather small and squat. It was completely rebuilt in 1884 to designs by G.E.Street.

The Georgian Church of St Mary's, considered to be the Mother Church of Southampton before it was completely rebuilt in 1878.

St Mary's Street was a bustling shopping street with many successful businesses. The Kingsland Tavern and market can be seen on the left.

St Mary's Church and the corner of Chapel Road and St Mary's Street. Originally a Saxon foundation, the church was repaired and rebuilt several times. As Victorian expansion encompassed this area of the town the church was renewed again with the addition of a spire transforming its previously squat appearance. The spire was completed in 1914 shortly before this picture was taken.

St Mary's Street 1910-12. Woodford and Far were already supplying equipment for motor vehicles, and next door to the Unicorn Pub, Walpole Herbal Chemists shows that alternative medicine was nothing new. Standing back behind iron railings is the Oddfellows Hall.

Opening of the new Central Stores, of Southampton Co-operative Society, in St Mary's Road, 11 March 1907.

From being a successful cycle manufacturers, Archlands moved to new premises in St Mary's Street and diversified into the manufacture of motorcycles. Mr William Ackland, and Mr Butler (in the side-car) are pictured on an Ackland machine around 1915.

552   THE SOUTHERN REFEREE   August 11, 1904

The "ACKLAND" SCORES.

Championships !

Records!

Handicaps!

The 25 Miles Championship
OF THE
SOUTHAMPTON ROVERS C.C.,
Held at WESTWOOD PARK on JULY 4th,
WAS WON BY
A. A. SPURRIER, ON HIS "ACKLAND,"
IN 1h. 11min. 34sec. BEING **RECORD** FOR THE TRACK,
T. GROVES BEING SECOND IN 1h. 11min. 35sec.,
H. H. ARNOLD THIRD IN 1h. 11min. 36sec.,
ALL RIDING "ACKLANDS."
ALSO THE 25 MILES HANDICAP OF ABOVE CLUB WAS WON BY
H. H. ARNOLD, A. A. SPURRIER BEING THIRD,
ALL ON "ACKLANDS."

W. Ackland, Cycle Manufacturer
AND REPAIRER,
52, ST. ANDREW'S ROAD,
SOUTHAMPTON.

Printed for the Proprietors at the "OBSERVER" Office, 31 Above Bar, Southampton, Saturday, August 11, 1904.

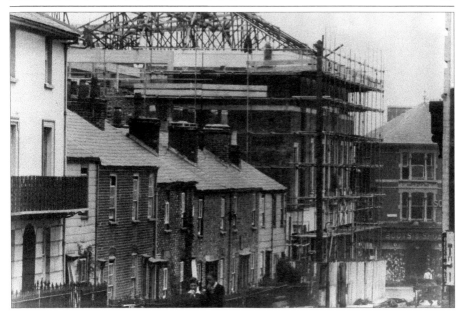

The new Co-operative store in St. Mary's Road, viewed from Compton Walk, under construction in 1934, by the Co-operative Wholesale Society Building Department. Southampton Co-operative Society started in 1887, and by 1950 it had 100 retail branches, a fleet of over 200 vehicles, employed 1,200 people and had an annual turnover of £4,000,000

St Mary's Road looking north 1908-10. The large Co-operative Stores at 122 and 123 had been opened with much pomp and ceremony in March 1907.

George Gillet's butchers in St Mary's Meat Market, Christmas 1934. Before home freezers were common many people waited until Christmas Eve to buy their turkey and often butchers in the meat market were still trading at midnight, by which time prices were much reduced!

South Hants Steam Laundry Company in Marsh Lane with three of their delivery vehicles. They were a substantial business employing 120 people during the 1890s and servicing hotels, schools, clubs and yachts. In an 1896 advertisement lady customers were invited to inspect the works on Thursdays from 11.00am and 1.00pm when all departments were in 'full work'.

Holy Trinity church, Kingsland, by Phillip Brannon. The artist himself wrote about the view in 1850, describing it thus: "It adjoins the Penitentiary, and forms a very pleasing scene, with the Dorchester Railway – constructed in the bed of the old canal, just in front,…" *54/1102*

The last nine Southampton Corporation working horses, just before their retirement in 1967.

Peartree Green

T HE village of Peartree Green, in the parish of St Mary Extra, was a small rural community on the Eastern bank of the river Itchen, connected to Southampton via a floating bridge. The church, known as Jesus Chapel, on the green, had been an 'overspill' church for St Mary's when the increased population of that ward meant that the mother church became too small. Although this was not entirely practical, due to the location of the village, it accounted for its inclusion in the parish of St Mary Extra.

Associated with the building of the church and of Peartree House around 1600 was Captain Richard Smith, who is believed to have financed both ventures. Although only a small 'country seat' with ten bedrooms, Peartree House was substantially modernised in the late eighteenth century with a crenellated stucco facade in the Gothic revival fashion. From the late 1880s it was the home of General Shrapnel, inventor of the Shrapnel shell.

By the late nineteenth century the village was supporting a board school, post office and several public houses and was described in the 1892 street directory as containing 'many handsome villas and houses, mostly occupied by the traders of Southampton'. More intense suburban development, however, did not take place until the 1920s and 1930s.

Peartree House, built by Captain Richard Smith around 1600, but with the addition of a crenellated facade, added in 1804 to keep up with the Gothic revival fashion. The house was also the nineteenth-century home of General Shrapnel.

The pear trees from which the village of Peartree Green took its name.

The Board School at Peartree Green next to Jesus Chapel. The school was mixed and large enough to accommodate 300 children although the average attendance during the 1890s was only 165. There was a mistress who lived at the school, an infant teacher and usually a 'pupil' teacher.

Bitterne and Bitterne Park

BITTERNE has been identified as the Roman settlement of Clausentum. Its site was first suggested by the historian and cartographer John Speed, and a number of Roman discoveries brought to light during the building of the first Northam Bridge in the 1790s seemed to support this theory. Despite continuing antiquarian interest in the site, it was not until part of Bitterne Manor estate was sold for development in the 1890s that the opportunity to explore the site further presented itself. The Society of Antiquaries of London commissioned a report on the threat to the site, but by the time it was published in 1902 much of the remainder of the bank and outer ditch had been removed to provide metalling for new roads.

Whilst it seems fairly certain that Bitterne is also the site of the Roman town of Clausentum and research from the 1950 onwards, has established this as an important military and commercial base with a substantial jetty and warehouse. Although there is some evidence of subsequent occupation, the withdrawal of the Roman legions in 410 eventually led to the re-location of the town into the Saxon port of Hamwic by the Saxons.

On part of the Clausentum site the substantial Bitterne Manor was built during the twelfth century. It was sometimes known as the Bishop's Palace, as it was in the ownership of Winchester Cathedral, and was often used by the Bishops of Winchester. By the seventeenth century it had declined in status, although it was still the centre of a large farm, but by the opening of the Northam Bridge in the 1790s it was serving as an inn. Both the manor and estate were sold for housing development to the National Land Corporation in 1899, and the house was badly damaged by enemy bombing in 1940. The derelict remains were finally acquired by the famous 'garden city' architect, Herbert Collins, in 1950, who sympathetically rebuilt the house to provide 14 new flats.

The suburb of Bitterne Park was the late nineteenth-century residential development promoted by the National Liberal Land Company. The Land Company erected the new Cobden Bridge in 1883, which was free of tolls, and this, together with the London and South Western Railway connection which had crossed the Itchen in 1866, enabled the company to promote the estate as the 'most charming' and 'most convenient' of all the Southampton suburbs.

Painting by Phillip Brannon, 1856, of a 'fanciful view' of Roman Southampton.

The toll gate on Lances Hill, Bitterne, *c.*1919. It was moved from its original position opposite Chessel Lodge because local people discovered they could make a short cut down Juniper Road and Beech Avenue and so avoid the halfpenny toll. The long brick wall on the left marked the boundary of the Chessel Estate, and the lady on the bicycle is believed to be a Miss Bailey, who was a teacher at Bitterne School.

Shops at Bitterne Park, *c.*1910.

Shirley

SHIRLEY, about two miles from the town, began life as a rural village on the Romsey Road. During the fifteenth century the manor came into the possession of Robert Whitehead, whose family retained it until the eighteenth century. Their name is preserved in Whithed Wood, which was originally Whitehead's Wood. The estate included several hundred acres along Hill Lane, known as Shirley Common and Shirley Warren, which was land with ancient rights allowing the taking of rabbits and small game.

A manor house called Withedwood was built from an existing farmhouse around 1820 and was the home of the Howard family until it was taken over by the shipbuilding Day family in the 1880s. The house became a boys' school in 1926 and a civil defence centre during World War Two after which it was requisitioned by the council and turned into flats. It was demolished in 1950.

A land dispute over the estate arose during the eighteenth century when the landowner, Gifford Warrine, was declared a lunatic by his appointed trustee. This resulted in the enclosure of much of the common and warren land which was sold as allotments, and allowed extensive residential development to proceed.

By the 1890s there was an overwhelming argument to include Shirley within the borough boundaries of Southampton. Most of its inhabitants worked in the town, but as a separate district, it had poor sewerage with a defective outfall at Four Posts Hill, no isolation hospital and no police force, which had led to the formation of a Garden Protection Society. These factors, together with increasing population pressure, made the benefits of inclusion obvious and Shirley was incorporated into Eaton in 1895. Many parts of the estate which had been leased for agriculture became ripe for development and roads such as Landguard, Arthur and Atherley were soon laid out with town villas and terraces, the building of which continued in stages through to the 1930s.

'Old Shirley Village' at the crossroads of Shirley High Street, Winchester Road and Romsey Road. Despite the 'Thatched House Inn' the redbrick suburban terraces have encroached some miles from the centre of the town.

The Old Shirley Tap, public house at the crossing of Winchester Road and Percy Road.

By the time these pictures were taken in 1915, Shirley had been incorporated into the Borough of Southampton and was rapidly loosing its market gardening and strawberry fields to make way for new housing projects.

A horse-drawn tram in Shirley High Street, outside the Shirley Temperance Hotel in the 1890s.

Tram number 15 at the Shirley terminus about 1910. Although the trams and tramlines had all gone by the 1950s, this part of the town survived the war remarkably unscathed and many of the Victorian and Edwardian buildings still remain.

Removing the tram tracks from Shirley High Street early in the 1950s. The city abandoned trams in favour of diesel buses in 1949. The last remaining route was the Floating Bridge to Shirley route which saw its very last tram run into the Shirley depot on 31 December 1949.

The opening of a branch of the public library on Shirley Road in 1893 was a growing indication of the importance of this area as a residential suburb of the town. The 1893 street directory declared that the library 'is well supplied with daily and weekly newspaper and has a library of about 7,000 volumes'.

The Atherley Cinema in Shirley Road was built in 1912. It pioneered the showing of "Cinemascope" films in Southampton, but ultimately became a bingo hall.

The successful butchery business of Edward Penfold at 40 High Street, Shirley. Taken around 1910 the turkeys and large bunches of mistletoe indicate that it was Christmas time.

Bristol Street Motor Company, 362 Shirley Road. *54/827*

William Gange outside his substantial Boot and Shoe manufacturing business at Oxford Buildings on the corner of Church Street and Shirley High Street. He also had another shop in East Street. *M5854*

Southampton football supporters at The Dell, during a match against Millwall in 1918. The Saints had begun in the 1880s as St Mary's Young Men's Christian Association, they began playing at The Dell, their own purpose-built ground, in 1898.

Portswood and Highfield

THE suburbs of Portswood and Highfield were developed on the estates of several of the country houses which had been established there during the late eighteenth century, when Southampton was at the height of its popularity as a spa resort.

Portswood, being closer to the centre of the town, probably developed its suburban setting first. Prior to World War One, the most significant building in the area, other than Bevois Mount House and the police station, was the Portswood tram depot. Originally built for horse trams, the depot later manufactured the city's electric trams, and provided significant local employment. Bevois Valley was a busy shopping centre by 1920 and local industry included the Winchester Brewery in Empress Road, together with a joinery works and a tobacco factory.

The children of the suburb were served by the Portswood Temporary Board School from 1899 until 1905: this was a single room designed to accommodate 140 pupils, but already taking 162 in its first year. Many of the children were from desperately poor families and had to be fed from a soup kitchen set up by the mistress, Miss Windebank, in the school. The new Portswood Infants' School, dating from 1846, was attached to the church, which was shared by other parishes. Taunton's School moved to Highfield from New Road in 1914, when Uplands House and part of the estate were acquired, although due to the outbreak of war, the school buildings were not completed and officially opened until 1927.

Undoubtedly the most important educational establishment in Highfield is the University. The Hartley Institute buildings on the High Street had long been considered too small for such a growing facility, and the present site, then known as Back Lane, was purchased, together with Highfield House, just before World War One.

Although building had commenced, and the first section completed, the site was requisitioned as a military hospital under the command of Dr R.E.Lauder, Southampton's Medical Officer of Health. A large number of wooden huts were built to serve as extra wards for the wounded coming back from the Western Front. Residential developments continued to expand throughout the 20th. Century with Council housing being built in Broadlands Road and Harefield Road. Later the "Flower" estates were built to the north of Burgess Road.

The Burgess Street, now Burgess Road toll gate. It stood at the bottom on the north side and was the home of the toll keeper Mr Pragnell when this picture was taken around 1900.
F.G.Bealing Collection.

The interior of one of the potting sheds of F.G.Bealings Nursery in Burgess Road around 1935. This considerable family business supplied plants and flowers to decorate the great liners regularly using the docks.

Southampton Horticultural Show, at the Ice Rink, part of the sports complexion Bannister Court Road, 1936.
Photograph from F.B.Bealing Collection.

Bevois Mount house originally built in 1723, was considerably enlarged when William Betts purchased in in 1844, although much of the estate was sold for building when Betts went bankrupt in the 1860s. The house became a girls private school, and was acquired by the Hartley Institute as a hostel for female students in 1900. During World War One it was used as a prisoner of war camp and finally a garage in the 1920s. It was demolished in 1939.

Houses in Ethelbert Avenue designed by the architect Herbert Collins famous for his involvement in 'garden city' design. He was instrumental in building small, well-layed out estates at affordable prices for the 'ordinary' people of Southampton.

Mr and Mrs Holdaway in the garden of their Herbert Collins home at 59 Ethelbert Avenue, in the late 1930s.

Scouts taking part in a shooting competition at Highfield Lodge in 1912. The scoutmaster on the right was Charles Godwin of Bitterne Scouts.

Highfield Church with Highfield Lane running across the picture, but almost obscured by trees, about the turn of the 20th. Century. The church was also known as Christ Church, Portswood, and was shared by both parishes. *M4502.*

Christmas, in the new university buildings at Highfield. The requisition of the buildings for use as a military hospital throughout World War One delayed the university's move to the site until 1919.

Despite its rural setting, the village of Swaythling was linked to the town by rail, the station having been opened in 1883.

Part of the new university campus at Highfield.

Suburban housing development can already be seen encroaching upon the country lane behind the children photographed in about 1910.

Millbrook

MILLBROOK, at the head of Southampton Water, and about two miles from the city, managed to retain its village character until after World War Two. Close to the borough boundary but not included until the 1920s, most of the inhabitants who did not work in the town had market gardening plots. The village had a railway station, and was well served by omnibuses, firstly horse-drawn and later motor-powered. Trams also ran from the town to the station between 1922 and 1935. The National School was built in 1825 and for a time the village even had two churches. Holy Trinity which was erected in 1874, and St Nicholas, which it replaced, but which remained in use for some time as a mortuary chapel.

The medieval church of St Nicholas was replaced as Millbrook's Parish Church by Holy Trinity in 1874. The old church was then used as a mortuary chapel. Millbrook, in spite of the Western Docks development in the early 1930s, was not absorbed within the municipal boundaries until 1954.

Although only two miles from Southampton, Millbrook remained a village until the 1930s when residential properties spread along Millbrook Road. It had however grown substantially, with a fourteen-fold increase in population to 17,777 between 1801 and 1891.

Thatched cottages and Four Posts Mission Room in Millbrook Road, near the site of the present railway station.

Southampton from Millbrook Shore. Millbrook was still a rural village two miles from the town.

Southampton central railway station, still with its clock tower in the early 1950s.

Dragon's teeth and knife rest anti-invasion road block defences on Millbrook Road in 1945.

Redbridge Village, four miles west of Southampton. Although it did not have a church it had a railway
station and large brewery.

The first Southampton Corporation motor bus, at Tanners brook, Millbrook in 1919.

The water mill at Woodmill on the Itchen, as rebuilt in about 1820. This was the third site of Walter Taylor's pioneer block making factory, having commenced his experiments in mechanising production in Westgate Street in the 1760s. He is also credited with adapting the watchmakers' circular saw to large-scale work.

Southampton airport in 1938. lack of a concrete runway at this time limited its use, although there was a Jersey airways service. The airport now has its on railway station, Southampton Parkway on this, the Southampton-Waterloo line.

ND - #0298 - 270225 - C0 - 234/156/12 - PB - 9781780913186 - Gloss Lamination